CRABTREE CONTACT

MOTO̶̶̶̶̶SS

Ben Johnson

🌱 Crabtree Publishing Company

www.crabtreebooks.com

**Crabtree Publishing
Company**
PMB 16A,
350 Fifth Avenue,
Suite 3308
New York, NY 10118

616 Welland Avenue,
St. Catharines, Ontario
L2M 5V6

Content development by
Shakespeare Squared

www.ShakespeareSquared.com

Published by Crabtree
Publishing Company © 2008

First published in Great Britain
in 2008 by ticktock Media Ltd,
2 Orchard Business Centre,
North Farm Road,
Tunbridge Wells, Kent, TN2 3XF

ticktock project editor:
 Ruth Owen
ticktock project designer:
 Sara Greasley
ticktock picture researcher:
 Lizzie Knowles

With thanks to: Series Editors Honor Head
and Jean Coppendale

Picture credits (t=top; b=bottom; c=centre;
l=left; r=right):
Steve Bardens/ actionplus: 4-5, 21b. Shelly
Castellano/ Icon SMI/ Corbis: 26-27. DPPI/
Actionplus: 29. Imagebroker/ Alamy: 25t.
Ben Johnson: 10-11. Martin Meissner/ AP/
PA Photos: 12-13. Aris Messinis/ AFP/ Getty
Images: 24-25. Phil Rees/ Rex Features: 23.
Sherman/ Getty Images: 7. Shutterstock:
OFC, 1, 2, 8, 14, 15, 16, 17, 18-19, 19t, 20,
21t, 28, 31.

Every effort has been made to trace copyright
holders, and we apologize in advance for any
omissions. We would be pleased to insert the
appropriate acknowledgments in any
subsequent edition of this publication.

Library and Archives Canada Cataloguing in Publication

Johnson, Ben, 1982-
    Motocross / Ben Johnson.

(Crabtree contact)
Includes index.
ISBN 978-0-7787-3764-3 (bound).
--ISBN 978-0-7787-3786-5 (pbk.)

    1. Motocross--Juvenile literature. I. Title. II. Series.

GV1060.12.J64 2008   j796.7'56   C2008-901210-0

Library of Congress Cataloging-in-Publication Data

Johnson, Ben.
  Motocross / Ben Johnson.
       p. cm. -- (Crabtree contact)
  Includes index.
  ISBN-13: 978-0-7787-3786-5 (pbk. : alk. paper)
  ISBN-10: 0-7787-3786-1 (pbk. : alk. paper)
  ISBN-13: 978-0-7787-3764-3 (reinforced library binding : alk. paper)
  ISBN-10: 0-7787-3764-0 (reinforced library binding : alk. paper)
  1. Motocross--Juvenile literature. I. Title.
  GV1060.12.J64 2008
  796.7'56--dc22
                                                              2008006260

CONTENTS

WARNING!

The moves and stunts featured in this book have been performed by experienced, highly trained motocross riders. Under no circumstances try them yourself! **You have been warned!**

Neither the publisher nor the author shall be liable for any bodily harm or damage to property whatsoever that may be caused or sustained as a result of conducting any of the activities featured in this book.

THE START

Motocross is one of the most exciting sports in the world.

Up to 40 riders on special motorbikes race against each other.

They race on dirt tracks in open country. A motocross track is about one mile (1,500 to 2,000 meters) long.

The tracks include huge hills and **drops**. There are fast, bumpy **straights** and tight corners.

There are big jumps.

This is motocross!

The first motocross races took place in the 1940s.

Special bikes were built for motocross from old road motorbikes.

The first motocross tracks didn't have many jumps because the bikes were heavy and not very strong. Also, the bikes had poor **acceleration**. But on a straight, they could go at about 80 miles per hour (129 kilometers per hour).

Tracks were built for fast riding. They had a lot of straights and fast corners.

The first motocross bikes were made entirely of metal. Some bikes weighed more than 400 pounds! (200 kilograms)

Modern motocross bikes weigh about 220 pounds (100 kilograms).

MIGHTY MACHINES

Modern motocross bikes have more powerful engines than bikes from the past had.

They have tougher **suspensions** and are much lighter. Modern bikes are made from lightweight aluminum and strong plastic.

This means the tracks can be rougher! They have more jumps and bigger jumps.

Modern tracks test the riders to the limit.

In the 1980s and 1990s, motocross became more and more popular. Today, thousands of people all over the world watch and take part in motocross races.

THE BIKE

Motocross bikes are very different from normal motorbikes. The engines in motocross bikes are built for power and speed.

Slim bodywork

The 2008 Yamaha YZ250F is one of the most powerful motocross bikes.

It has six **gears**.

It has 13 inches (33 centimeters) of suspension at the front and back. This soaks up the impact of the big jumps and rough bumps on the track.

Chunky **tread**

Tires with chunky treads help the bike grip the loose dirt.

Lightweight frame

Powerful engine

Tough suspension

IT'S TOUGH!

Motocross is one of the
toughest sports in the world.

Riders must train hard and be very fit and strong to compete.

Sometimes bad crashes happen.

SAFETY GEAR

Riders wear a lot of special gear and clothing when they race.

A helmet protects the head in a crash. It stops dirt and rocks from hitting the face. Goggles protect the eyes.

Helmet

Goggles

Armor is worn under or over a rider's jersey. It protects his or her chest and back from flying dirt and rocks.

Riders wear special race jerseys, gloves, and jeans. They are made of tough material. The material is very light and lets the rider move easily and not become too hot.

Knee braces protect their knees in a fall.

Riders wear leather boots with hard plastic protectors. The boots keep their feet and legs safe from damage in falls — and from other riders!

THE RACE

Racers live for the time they line up for the start of a race.

The starter holds up a 30-second board. There are 30 seconds to go before the race starts.

The starter holds up another board. There are **five seconds** to go before the race starts.

The riders get their bikes in gear.

Then they are off!

The racers charge into the first turn together. The bikes must pull through the deep dirt.

This is the most exciting and **dangerous** part of the race.

SPEED AND SKILL

The early stages of a race are frantic. Riders fight over top positions.

The bikes power up fast to push over the jumps.

Only the most skillful riders are able to attack the track and different jumps at full speed.

They quickly find their way to the lead positions.

THE FINISH

The race lasts for 30 minutes. The track gets very rough by the end of the race.

The riders start to feel physically and mentally tired.

Riders who have trained hard and are very fit can pass tired rivals. The top riders can keep up their speed for the entire race.

A rider may become so tired that he or she loses control of the bike.

What does it take to win?

Focus
Energy
Strength
Talent
Skill

and maybe some
Good luck!

SUPERCROSS

Supercross is a more spectacular form of motocross racing.

Supercross takes place on specially built tracks inside big stadiums.

Supercross is all about huge jumps and tight turns. These make the races more exciting and thrilling, and **WOW** the huge crowds.

The races are short and
action-packed.

Racers have to ride very hard to overtake other riders and finish in the top spots. Supercross tracks are smaller than normal motocross tracks are.

Stadium

Track

Riders

JUMPS

Riders need perfect timing and balance to handle big jumps.

Jumps give riders many chances to pass other riders. As they fly over the jumps, riders try to take a better route than their rivals and overtake them.

Long sections of jumps are called **rhythm sections**. The closely spaced bumps are known as **whoops**.

This is a big **triple jump**. Riders need a lot of speed to get over more than one jump at a time.

Rhythm section

Whoops

FREESTYLE

Freestyle is the most extreme type of motocross. It's also the most dangerous.

Riders do not race in freestyle. Instead, they perform giant jumps and amazing tricks on their bikes.

Take-off ramp

Riders use giant ramps
to help them get as much
height as possible.

TRICKS

Good freestyle riders often do more than one trick as they fly through the air.

Here a freestyle rider performs two tricks at once. This move is called a

Seat Grab Hart Attack.

A seat grab is when a rider grabs hold of the bike's saddle.

A Hart Attack is when a rider throws his or her legs into the air above his or her head. This trick was invented by rider Carey Hart.

A rider gets upside down as he performs the backflip. This is one of the hardest and most dangerous freestyle tricks of all. Only the best riders can tackle this move.

Motocross really is incredible!

acceleration The rate at which a bike increases its speed

drops Steep slopes from the tops of hills that make the course more challenging

gears Mechanical parts of the bike that help it accelerate and produce more power when approaching jumps

rhythm sections Long sections of differently spaced jumps

straights The fastest sections of a motocross track. Straights are not long, but they are difficult because the ground is rough and riders must hang on tight.

suspension The suspension is one of the most important parts of a motocross bike. It acts like a cushion so the riders don't feel all the bumps of the track. It also helps the tires grip the track.

tread The surface of a tire. The tread on a motocross tire has thick rubber blocks that dig into the dirt to push the bike forward.

triple jump When riders jump a huge distance in the air over a jump that features three dirt ramps in a row. The best riders jump all three ramps in one go.

whoops A section of track that features a long series of large human-made bumps. The riders attack them at great speed so they can skim across the tops of the bumps.

- Getting started in motocross is easier than you think. There are motocross schools and camps located all over the world. Skilled instructors can help future racers get a proper start.

- On the website of the American Motorcyclist Association (AMA) you can find out where your local clubs meet. Also, check out the **want to race** section.

http://www.ama-cycle.org

MOTOCROSS ONLINE

http://www.racerxill.com
http://www.transworldmotocross.com
http://www.motocrossmx1.com
http://www.womensmotocrossassociation.com

Printed in the U.S.A